Percussion

Elizabeth Sharma

Thomson Learning
New York

Books in the series

Brass	Strings
Keyboards	The Voice
Percussion	Woodwinds

First published in the
United States in 1993 by
Thomson Learning
115 Fifth Avenue
New York, NY 10003

First published in 1992 by
Wayland (Publishers) Ltd

Cataloging-in-Publication Data applied for

ISBN 1-56847-113-0

Printed in Belgium by Casterman, s.a.,
Bound in Italy by L.E.G.O.

Contents

When you were a baby, you were probably given a rattle to play with. You probably sometimes banged your spoon or cup against the table. You might even have had a small toy drum.

People clap their hands when they are enjoying a **rhythmic** piece of music. We all enjoy making rhythmic sounds from an early age, and this is why there are more percussion instruments in the world than any other kind of instrument.

(Below) These young performers are playing large Japanese drums.

This is an Egyptian band. See if you can pick out the percussion instruments. The man standing near the back is playing tiny finger cymbals.

Percussion instruments are instruments that are played by striking them with the hands or a stick, or by knocking one part of the instrument against another.

Percussion instruments can be as large as the Japanese drum or as small as the Egyptian finger cymbals.

Hands and feet make the rhythm complete

Drum sets can be played to add exciting rhythms to popular and rock music. They are used in jazz, steel band, and many other kinds of music.

The way the drum set is arranged makes it possible for one person to play all the instruments. Playing the drum set properly is very difficult. You have to be able to work different instruments at the same time, using both hands and both feet.

This drummer plays in a popular band.

Could you learn to play the drum set? Practice by walking in place and counting like this:

| right foot | left foot | right foot | left foot |
| 1 | 2 | 3 | 4 |

Clap when you step on the left foot, on **beat** 2 and beat 4. Now ask a partner to play the tambourine:

| 1 and | 2 and | 3 and | 4 and |

If you have a drum set at school, try pressing the bass-drum pedal with your right foot and the hi-hat pedal with your left foot.

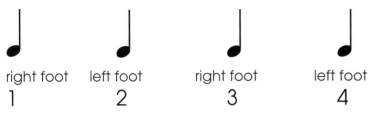

right foot	left foot	right foot	left foot
1	2	3	4

Strike the snare drum on beats 2 and 4 with your left stick. When you can do that, play the hi-hat cymbal with your right stick:

1 and   2 and   3 and   4 and

This girl is playing the snare drum with her left hand and the hi-hat cymbal with her right hand. Her right foot presses the bass-drum pedal. Her left foot presses the hi-hat pedal.

Rhythm on the move

In a marching band, the percussion section makes sure that all the other musicians play and march in time. Percussion instruments also make the music more exciting. The various instruments of a drum set are each played by a different person.

One person carries the bass drum on a strap around one shoulder, hitting it first on one side, then the other. There are usually several people playing snare drums. Others clash the cymbals, holding one in each hand.

These soldiers are in a Scottish marching band. The man on the right is playing a bass drum. The others are playing snare drums.

Have you ever seen a parade where soldiers play their instruments on horseback? This is called a mounted military band. The horses have to be very well trained so that they are not frightened by the loud music. The riders control the horses with their knees. This keeps their hands free to play their instruments.

The kettledrums hang from either side of the drummer's horse. They can be tuned to different notes to match the music being played by the rest of the band.

This is a mounted military band in England. The second horse has kettledrums tied onto it.

Percussion joins the orchestra

When orchestral music is loud and exciting, or frightening, the percussion section adds the finishing touch. Composers use percussion instruments to create dramatic special effects.

There are usually three or four percussion players who may be called upon to play any of these instruments:

Here are some percussion players in a youth orchestra. Which percussion instruments can you see? The girl is waiting for the right moment to play the tambourine.

timpani (the larger
   orchestral version
   of kettledrums)
bass drum
snare drum
cymbals
gong
castanets
triangle
tambourine
woodblock
xylophone
marimba
glockenspiel
tubular bells
. . .and others

This girl is playing the timpani. Each drum is tuned to a different note.

Percussion instruments are only played at certain times in the music, unlike the stringed instruments, which are played most of the time.

Before the orchestra begins to play, the percussion players must figure out which one of them is going to play each instrument. They have to concentrate very hard so that they do not lose their place in the music. They must make sure they play at the right moment.

Good vibrations

All sound depends on **vibrations**. When you hit the skin of a drum, the air inside and around the drum is made to vibrate. This produces the sound.

When you hit a triangle, the metal vibrates, although you cannot see it happening. This makes the sound continue after the triangle has been struck. If you hold the triangle across the corner where there is a gap, and hit it again, you will not hear a clear, ringing sound. This is because you are stopping the vibration.

Try the same experiment with a cymbal. Hit it with a padded stick,

When this girl hits the cymbal, it continues to vibrate for a long time.

and let it vibrate freely and echo.
Now hit it again while holding the rim
of the cymbal. What happens?

These boys have covered one can with plastic wrap and another with cloth. They are deciding which one makes a better drum sound.

Percussion instruments need to be **resonant**. If you cover the **barrel** of a drum with a piece of cloth instead of tightly stretched skin or plastic, it will not produce a clear sound. The cloth is not resonant because it does not cause the air inside or around the drum to vibrate properly. The air escapes through the weave of the cloth.

Try this by covering an empty cookie tin or bowl with cloth, and tapping it with a drumstick. Then cover the bowl or tin with tightly stretched kitchen plastic wrap and tap it again.

Note or noise?

Many percussion instruments play a sound rather than a musical note. Try hitting a tambourine, striking a woodblock, or clashing some cymbals, and then singing the note they make. Instruments that make sounds that you cannot sing are called **unpitched** percussion.

All over the world, people make unpitched percussion instruments from things they find around them.

This is a group of musicians in Gambia. Some of them are playing unpitched percussion instruments made from pieces of wood. Instruments like this are called clappers.

Remember the baby rattle? The sound is produced by small, hard objects being shaken inside a hollow shell. This is how maracas are made.

Cabaca

A cabaca (say "cabassa") is a South American instrument with beads threaded on a net of string around a hollow shell. The hollow shell is made from a hard-skinned fruit called a gourd. When the cabaca is shaken, the beads vibrate against the gourd.

Look around your home and see what you can find to make some unpitched percussion instruments. Remember to ask permission before you use anything. You could fill plastic bottles with corn, rice, or lentils to make maracas. Clappers can be made from two small pieces of hard wood that you knock against each other.

A pair of maracas

Pitched percussion

Some percussion instruments have a definite **pitch**. They are called pitched percussion.

You can tune a set of timpani or kettledrums so that the notes they play fit in with the music played by the rest of the orchestra. You can play tunes on instruments like the xylophone or marimba. These instruments have notes made of resonant hard wood. Small blocks produce high notes, and larger blocks produce lower notes.

This girl is playing a xylophone, and this boy is playing a glockenspiel. They are listening to the difference between the high notes and the low notes.

The glockenspiel is similar to the xylophone but it has metal notes. In some marching bands, small glockenspiels are held upright on the players' shoulders.

Tubular bells are hung from a large frame. You can make your own set of tubular bells. Collect five large glass bottles or large drinking glasses, and fill them to different levels with water. Hit them softly with a xylophone beater or drumstick. See if you can **tune** them to some piano notes. You could play notes to go with a xylophone or recorder **melody**, or you could make up your own melody.

This boy has filled five bottles with water colored with food dye. He is tapping them with a drumstick to play different notes.

These Gambian drummers are playing drums covered with animal skin. They are like the drums played in ancient times.

From ancient times, people have signaled to each other by beating on hollow logs that were sometimes covered at the ends with animal skin. These instruments were also used to accompany singing and dancing, and for celebrations.

In some African countries and other parts of the world, repeated drum rhythms can make some people go into a **trance**. They are believed to be in contact with their **ancestors** through the playing of the ancient drum rhythms.

The ancient Greeks and Romans used drum rhythms to accompany their marching armies. Armies have marched to drum beats ever since.

When the rulers of ancient times wanted to cross the sea, they used sailboats, or they forced their slaves to row them in boats with huge oars. The slaves were seated in lines on either side of the boat, sometimes on several different levels. A drummer would play to keep them all rowing in time together.

This picture shows a Roman warship. The slaves had to row it with oars. On some boats there would have been a drummer to help them to row in time together.

The rhythm of words

When someone speaks, their words make a rhythm, and the pitch of their voice goes up and down. Some African languages, as well as the Chinese language, are said to be tonal. This means that the pitch of the voice is as important as the words spoken. The same word, spoken with a different rise or fall of the voice, can mean something quite different.

In Nigeria and some other African countries, expert drummers can **imitate** the rhythm, and the rise and fall of the voice, on their drums. It sounds exactly like speech to anyone who understands the language being imitated.

These men in Nigeria are playing talking drums. The strings on the drums are used to change the pitch of the note played.

The instruments used for this are called talking drums. They are shaped like an hourglass. The drummer uses the strings at the sides to tighten or loosen the skin to make a higher or a lower sound.

Talking drums are used to send messages or to praise important people during celebrations. They can also tell dancers which steps to perform.

You can use a set of bongo drums, or any drums of different pitches, as talking drums. Imitate the sound and rhythm of your classmates' names, and ask them to guess whose names you are playing.

These drummers are trying to make their drums "talk." They are imitating the sounds of their names.

The words of rhythm

This Indian man is playing the tabla. He is using his fingers and wrists to play the particular notes he wants.

Tabla are the drums played in Indian music. There are two drums in a set of tabla. The larger, played by the left hand, plays the lower sounds. The player can alter the pitch by pressing with the wrist while playing drum strokes with the fingers. Good players can produce a whole **scale**.

The right-hand drum is smaller. It can produce many different, and higher, sounds. Some sound almost bell-like.

Each different stroke on both drums, using combinations of both hands and all fingers, has a name. Tabla teachers **recite** the names of the strokes for their students to play. These names are called bols, which is the Hindi word for "words."

The gongs of gamelan

In Indonesia, traditional music is played by a gamelan, an orchestra made up mainly of percussion instruments. A gamelan contains sets of bronze gongs, xylophones, and metallophones. Metallophones are large xylophones with metal notes.

The gamelan plays a very important part in social life, and accompanies weddings, dances, and shadow puppet plays. Every village has its own gamelan, which is kept in an open hut in the center of the village.

This is a gamelan orchestra in Indonesia. There are several metallophones. You can see a man playing a bronze gong at the front.

Sunny steel

Have you heard the happy sound of a steel band? It makes people think of the sunny Caribbean.

Steel drums, or pans, as they are called, were invented in Trinidad around the time of World War II. People made them from empty oil drums left by the American troops.

Here is a steel band. Notice the different sizes of the pans.

The largest pans, made from whole oil drums, produce the bass notes. Some middle-sized drums are used to play **chords** and rhythms. The smallest pans are for playing the melodies.

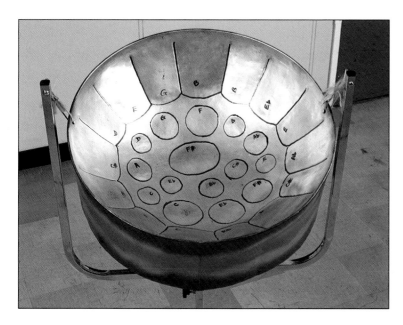

This is a soprano steel pan, sometimes called a first tenor. The notes are marked on the pan to help the player.

Look at the notes on a **soprano** pan, sometimes called a first tenor pan. They are not arranged in a scale like on a piano or xylophone. Different pan makers arrange their notes in different orders.

The steel pans are the only widely used new musical instrument other than electronic instruments to have been invented in the last fifty years. They are different from any other instrument, and they are a very good example of recycling.

Live Music!

If you march or dance to music, you have to be able to hear a strong, regular beat.

Western music is made up of small sections called bars, and the first beat in every bar is usually the strongest. Each bar has the same number of beats in it. In the United States, notes written like this – ♩ – are called quarter notes, and in England they are called crotchets. The $\frac{4}{4}$ numbers show that there must be the value of four quarter notes in each bar.

These girls in Zimbabwe are dancing to music. They can hear a regular beat from the metallophones behind them.

Try learning to read these rhythm patterns by saying the colors, or by playing them on different instruments.

$\frac{4}{4}$

red	red	red	red		red	red	red	red	
1	2	3	4		1	2	3	4	

$\frac{4}{4}$

green green green green
1 2 3 4   1 2 3 4

$\frac{4}{4}$

blue - oo - oo - oo   blue - oo - oo -- oo
1   2   3   4   1   2   3   4

$\frac{4}{4}$

yellow yellow yellow yellow   yellow yellow yellow yellow
1 and 2 and 3 and 4 and   1 and 2 and 3 and 4 and

$\frac{4}{4}$

pur - ple   pur - ple   pur - ple   pur - ple
1 2   and 3 4   and   1 2   and 3 4   and

Now try mixing up the colors and rhythm notes and making up your own rhythm patterns like this:

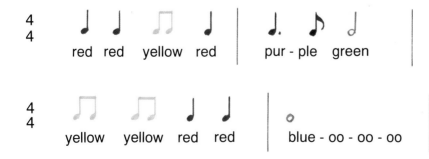

$\frac{4}{4}$

red red yellow red   pur - ple green

$\frac{4}{4}$

yellow yellow red red   blue - oo - oo - oo

A class band

Play properly, or your teacher might say you should be a class banned!

Collect together enough instruments for the whole class. Remember your homemade instruments, too. Group them according to the sounds they make.

1 Drum sounds
2 Cymbals
3 Bell sounds, such as triangles, Indian bells, bottles
4 Tambourine sounds
5 Woodblock sounds
6 Maracas and shakers

drum

shaker

tambourine

cymbals

woodblocks

triangle

Make up a short rhythm pattern for each group of instruments. Put on a suitable record, CD, or cassette, and play your rhythm patterns with the music. Decide which groups of instruments sound good together.

Now try making up some tunes of your own on the xylophone or glockenspiel, and organize your class band to accompany it.

These people are playing percussion instruments to accompany music from the cassette player.

Glossary

Ancestors   A person's relatives who lived a long time ago—long before their great-grandparents.

Barrel   The body of a drum, over which the skin is stretched.

Beat   A sound made over and over in a regular rhythm.

Chords   Groups of notes that are played together to produce an agreeable sound.

Imitate   To copy exactly.

Melody   The correct musical term for a tune.

Pitch   How high or low a note sounds.

Recite   To repeat words from memory.

Resonant   Able to produce a clear, ringing sound.

Rhythmic   Having a regular beat.

Scale   A group of musical notes going up or down at fixed intervals.

Soprano   The highest-pitched instrument in a family of instruments.

Trance   A dazed state in which a person might be dreaming or having visions.

Tune   To adjust to a certain pitch.

Unpitched   An instrument that does not produce a particular musical note.

Vibrations   When something shakes very quickly back and forth, it is said to vibrate. The movements are called vibrations.

Finding out more

1.   Why not listen to some percussion music?
African drum music: *The Drums of Passion Invocation* by Babatunde Olatunji
Orchestral percussion: *Also Sprach Zarathustra* by Richard Strauss
Mars from *The Planets* by Gustav Holst
Tabla: Records by Ustad Alla Rakha and Zakir Hussain
Tubular bells: *The 1812 Overture* by Tchaikovsky – the part when the Bells of Moscow ring out in triumph
Xylophone: *Dance Macabre* by Saint-Saens

2.   Watch concerts on television. There are often programs showing music from around the world.

3.   Try to hear some live music. Look for marching bands and parades. Many areas have youth orchestras and bands and would like to have more people at their concerts. Sometimes, musicians from around the world give performances as part of local festivals. Look for posters in your library and ask the librarians.

Useful books

Berger, Melvin. *The Science of Music*. New York: HarperCollins, 1989.
Greene, Carol. *Music*. Chicago: Childrens Press, 1983.
Mundy, Simon. *The Usborne Story of Music*. Tulsa: EDC, 1980.
Pillar, Marjorie. *Join the Band!*. New York: HarperCollins, 1992.
Wiseman, Ann. *Making Musical Things*. New York: Macmillan, 1979.

Index

Page numbers in **dark type** indicate subjects shown in pictures as well as in the text.

Acknowledgments

The photographs in this book were provided by: J. Allan Cash, 18, 24; C. M. Dixon, 19; East Sussex County Council, 10, 11; Jimmy Holmes, 4 (below); James Morris, 20; Panos Pictures (P. Harrison), 23; Photri, 4 (above); Picturepoint, 9; Rex Features (Gardner), 6; Peter Sanders, 5, 22; Tony Stone Worldwide (Bob Thomas), 8, (H. Kavanagh), 14; Topham (M. Mann), 26; Wayland Picture Library (Isabel Lilly), 12, (Zul Mukhida), 17, (all Garry Fry), cover, 7, 13, 16, 21, 25, 29.   Artwork: Creative Hands, 15, 27, 28.